9

P9-EJZ-107

DO THE RIGHT THING!

FRIENDSHIP

Written by Eric Suben
Illustrated by Barbara Lanza

ROURKE BOOK CO., INC.
VERO BEACH, FL 32964

© 1999 Rourke Book Co., Inc.

All rights reserved. No part of this book may be reproduced or utilized in any form or by any means, electronic or mechanical including photocopying, recording, or by any information storage and retrieval system without permission in writing from the publisher.

Printed in the United States of America.

Library of Congress Cataloging-in-Publication Data

Suben, Eric.
    Friendship / Eric Suben.
       p.   cm. — (Doing the right thing)
Summary: Simple text and illustrations describe how people become friends and give examples of how friends behave.
    ISBN 1-55916-231-7
    1. Friendship—Juvenile literature. [1. Friendship.   I. Title.
II. Series.
BJ1533.F8S92   1999
177'.62—dc21
                                                   98-48392
                                                         CIP
                                                         AC

FRIENDSHIP

4

Being a friend starts with liking someone who likes you, too. Friends spend time together, play together, and share with each other.

Sometimes you first meet a friend because you go to the same school or live on the same street.

You tell your friend his new hat is cool.
You want him to feel good.

You help your friend carry her backpack
to school when she has a broken leg.

9

Sometimes you can make a stranger into a friend. Say, "hello" to the new girl at school. Help her find her way to class.

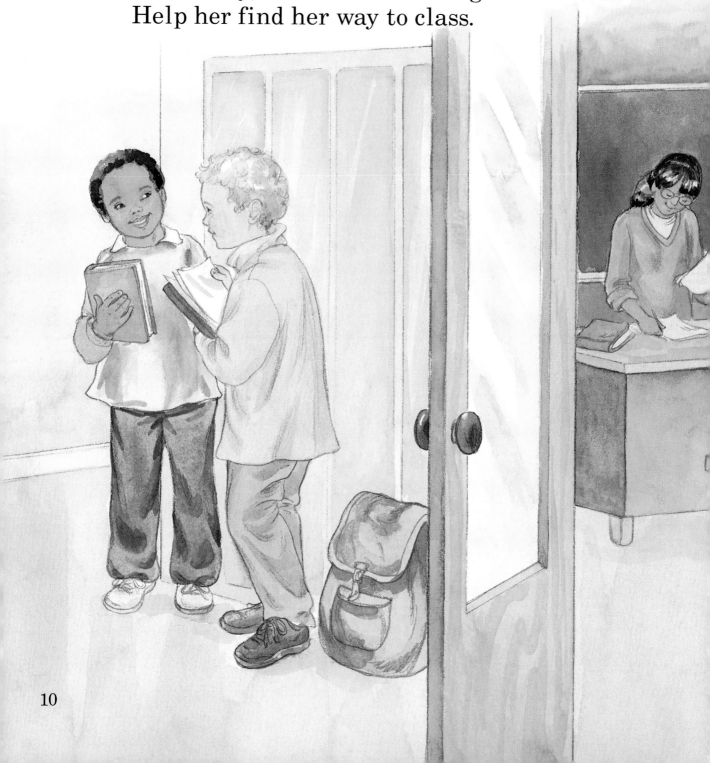

11

Introduce your friends to each other.
You may help them become friends, too.

Having a group of friends is fun when
everyone plays together.

You are nice to your friend even when he makes mistakes. You say, "Everyone makes mistakes."

You tell your friend when she does well
in the school play.

Invite a friend to play at your house.

You can help your friend with her
math homework.

A sleepover can make you and your friend
feel extra close.

18

You are a good friend when you ask your friend why he is sad, or when you try to make him laugh.

Your friends do not all have to be children.
Grown-ups such as your parents and teachers
are your friends because they help you and
care for you.

THIRD GRADE
CLASS PROJECT

Your brother and sisters are your friends because
they play with you and understand you.

A pet can be your friend, too.

You share your secrets with your friend.
Show him your special clubhouse!

You feel proud when your best friend
wins the race.

Your friend is still your friend even though she likes other people, too.

Friends are friends even when they
are not together. You can keep in
touch by talking on the telephone
or writing letters.

You can meet friends in many different places.
Summer camp is one place to make new friends.

Your friend can cheer you up if you hear
strange noises in the night.

Your friend may move away, but you can get together again. A good friend always remains a friend.

You Can Be a Friend!

These steps can help you be a good friend. But do NOT write in this book; use a sheet a paper.

1. **Who is your friend now?**
   Write 1-3 names.

   Who would you like to have as a friend?
   Write 1-3 more names.

2. **How can you show friendship?**
   Write one idea that you like from this book.
   How do you know when someone wants to be your friend?
   Write these ideas.
   Write your very own idea for showing friendship.

3. **Draw a star beside the 3 ideas (in step 2) that you like best.**

4. **Choose to start now.** Show someone you care before you go to bed tonight.

5. **Keep at it.** Show the person often that you want to be friends. Show her or him in different ways.

6. **Think about each of your friends.**
   How are they different from you?
   How are they like you?

7. **Say, "I am a good friend."**
   Say it many times every day.